The Original Witness

A Poetic Tribute for Lives Lost in the Texas Flood

Lisa K. Pelto

Published by
Concierge Publishing Services
Omaha, Nebraska
www.ConciergePublishingServices.com

First edition - Large Print
July 2025

ISBN: 978-1-936840-21-2

Proceeds from this publication will be donated to organizations assisting those affected by the 2025 Texas floods.

For those left behind in Texas—

May your grief be seen.
May your memories be honored.
And may something in these words
stand beside you,
quiet and steady,
as you find your way through the after.

The Original Witness

It simply must be aware
that we can't live without it.
There is no life,
no seed,
no bloom
without water.

But our need

does not

earn its mercy.

It doesn't need to know
the name of the child
or her dreams.
It doesn't even need to know
who is left behind,
because it's already
moving too fast,
stealing away
with someone who is loved.

It hummed to the banks
with the same tune it sang
when the children
dipped their toes in
hours before,
splashing,
unaware they were
touching the thing
that would not spare them.

It takes the path of least resistance,

not out of malice,

but because it has no choice.

Because getting

from up there

to down there

is all it was made to do.

There is no intention.

Only flow.

Only the innocence of water,

present for every ending,

and each beginning.

Pushing forward without memory.

It does not choose what it carries.

It does not ask permission.

It simply follows gravity's law,

fluid and final.

I was taught to bless myself

with holy water,

as if that made me

safe from harm,

as if water knows

how to tell

the difference

between good and evil.

We may beg it to be merciful,
but water keeps no promises.
It lingers for nothing.
It does not reason,
cannot apologize.
It leaves what it leaves.
And takes what it wants.

And if it bargains with your grief,

let your tears fall freely.

Perhaps that teardrop

was once a snowflake

atop a mountain peak,

or morning dew

on a cactus at dawn,

or relief on the cracked lips

of someone saved

a hundred years ago.

The tears you weep now

will someday return

to wash the hands

of those who mourn,

joined by the tears

of those who left before,

flowing ever forward

in the innocence

of water.

A Note from the Author

Thank you for reading

The Original Witness.

Proceeds from your purchase

will be donated to trusted

Texas flood relief organizations.

Your support is appreciated.

www.ingramcontent.com/pod-product-compliance
Lightning Source LLC
LaVergne TN
LVHW091237080426
835509LV00009B/1322